COMETS AND ASTEROIDS

By Rosie Rowntree

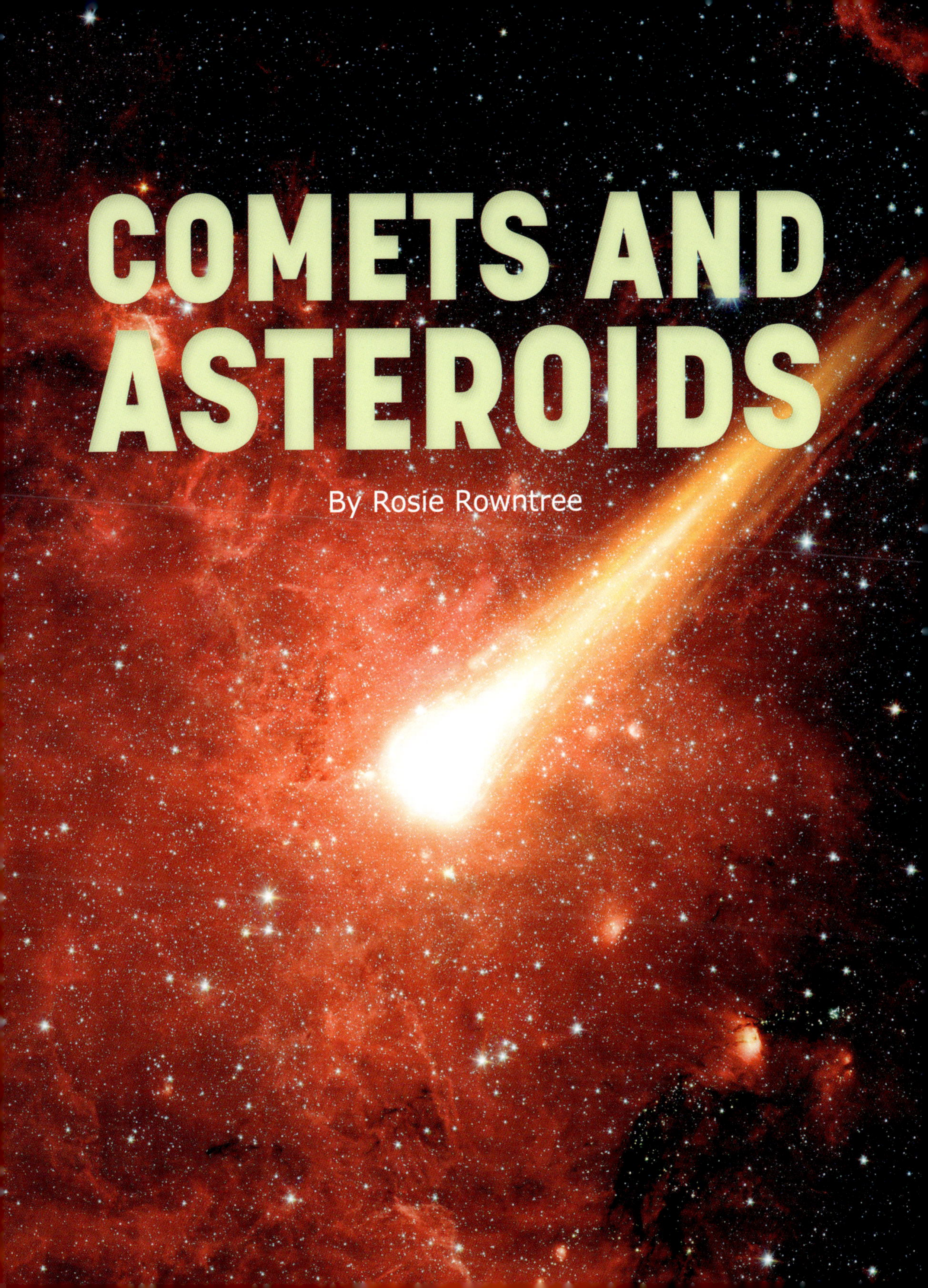

CONTENTS

The Solar System 4
What is an Asteroid? 6
Finding Asteroids 8
Hunting for Asteroids 10
Asteroids and Earth 12
What is a Comet? 14
Finding Comets 16
What Can We See? 18
Exploring Comets and Asteroids 20
What's Next? 22
Glossary 24

HUNGRY TOMATO

First published in 2026 by Hungry Tomato Ltd
F15, Old Bakery Studios, Blewetts Wharf, Malpas Road,
Truro, Cornwall, TR1 1QH, UK.

A CIP catalog record for this book is available from the British Library.

ISBN 9781835691038

Manufactured in the USA

Discover more at
www.hungrytomato.com

Front cover image is an edited image of an asteroid.
Title page image is an edited image of an asteroid.
Contents page image is an artist's impression of an asteroid.

Words in **BOLD** can be found in the glossary.

THE SOLAR SYSTEM

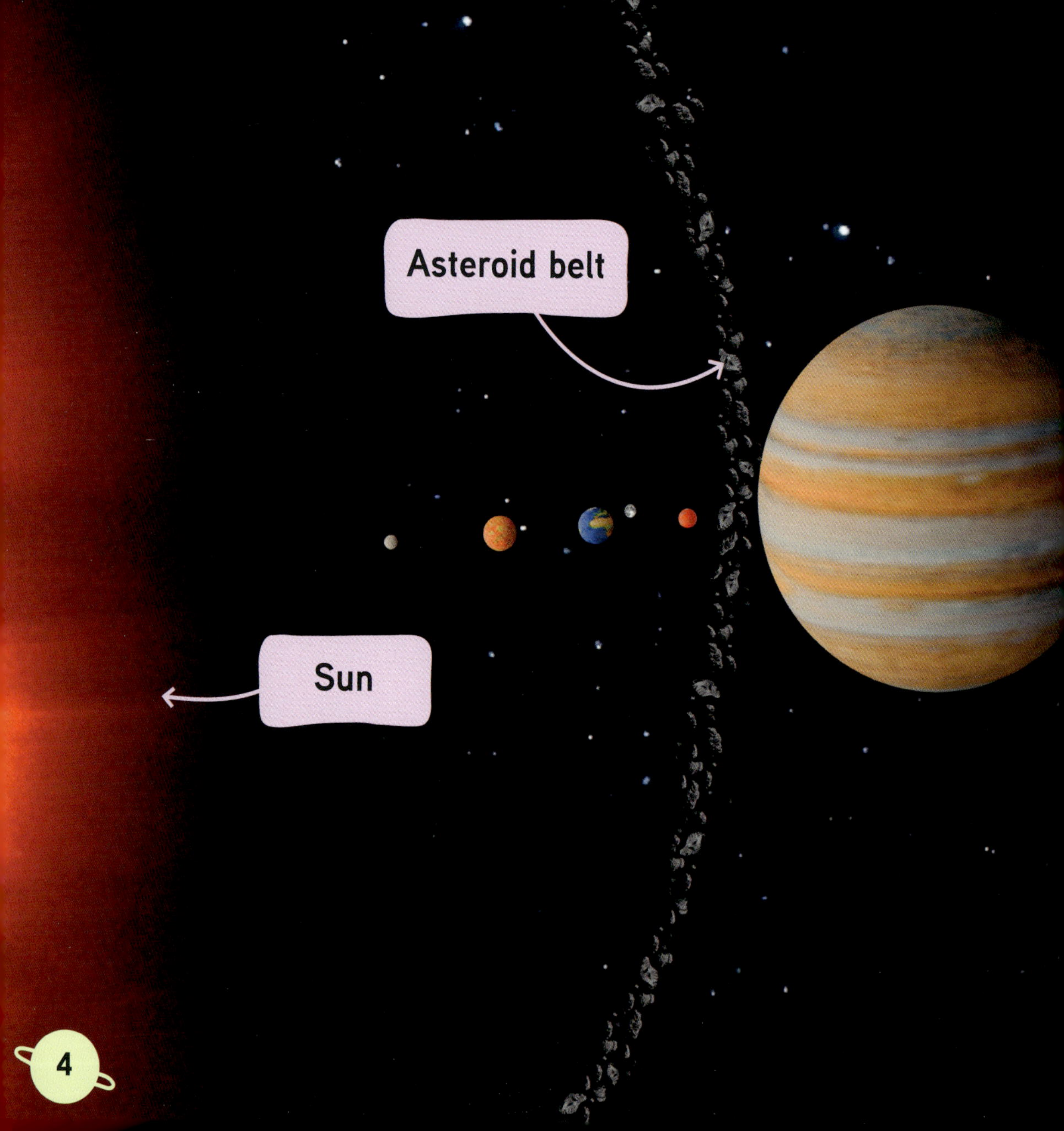

Kuiper Belt

The **solar system** was formed billions of years ago. It started as a spinning disk of **gas** and dust.

Comet

Most of this gas and dust formed the the Sun, planets, and **moons**. Smaller, leftover bits stuck together to create **comets** and **asteroids**.

WHAT IS AN ASTEROID?

Asteroids are small, rocky objects that **orbit** the Sun. They come in all shapes and sizes.

The largest known asteroid in the solar system is called Vesta. As well as being the largest asteroid, it is also the brightest. It can sometimes be seen from Earth using only the human eye!

Most asteroids are not as round as Vesta – or as big! They are usually a strange bumpy shape.

FINDING ASTEROIDS

Most asteroids are found in the **asteroid belt** between Mars and Jupiter.

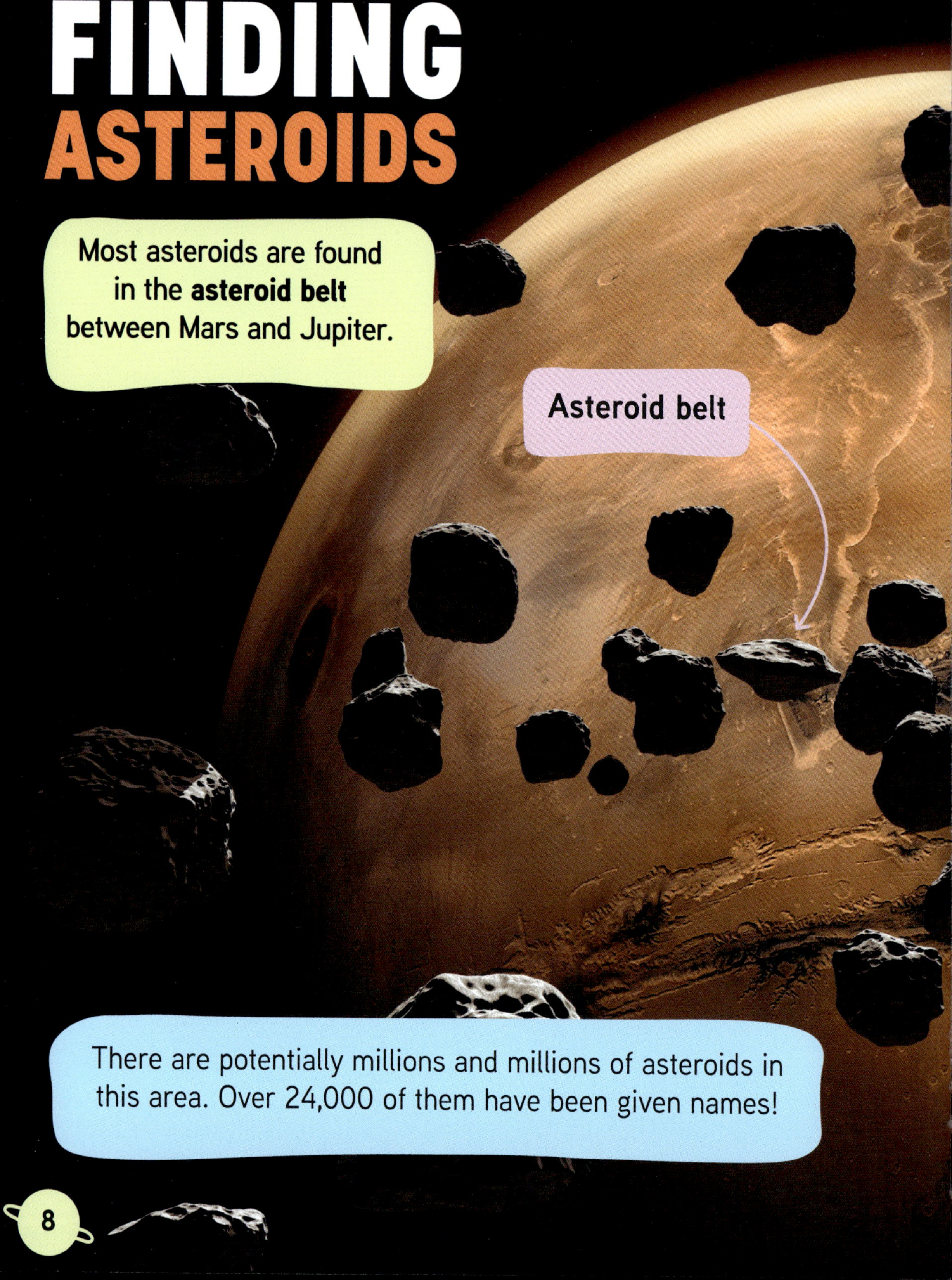

There are potentially millions and millions of asteroids in this area. Over 24,000 of them have been given names!

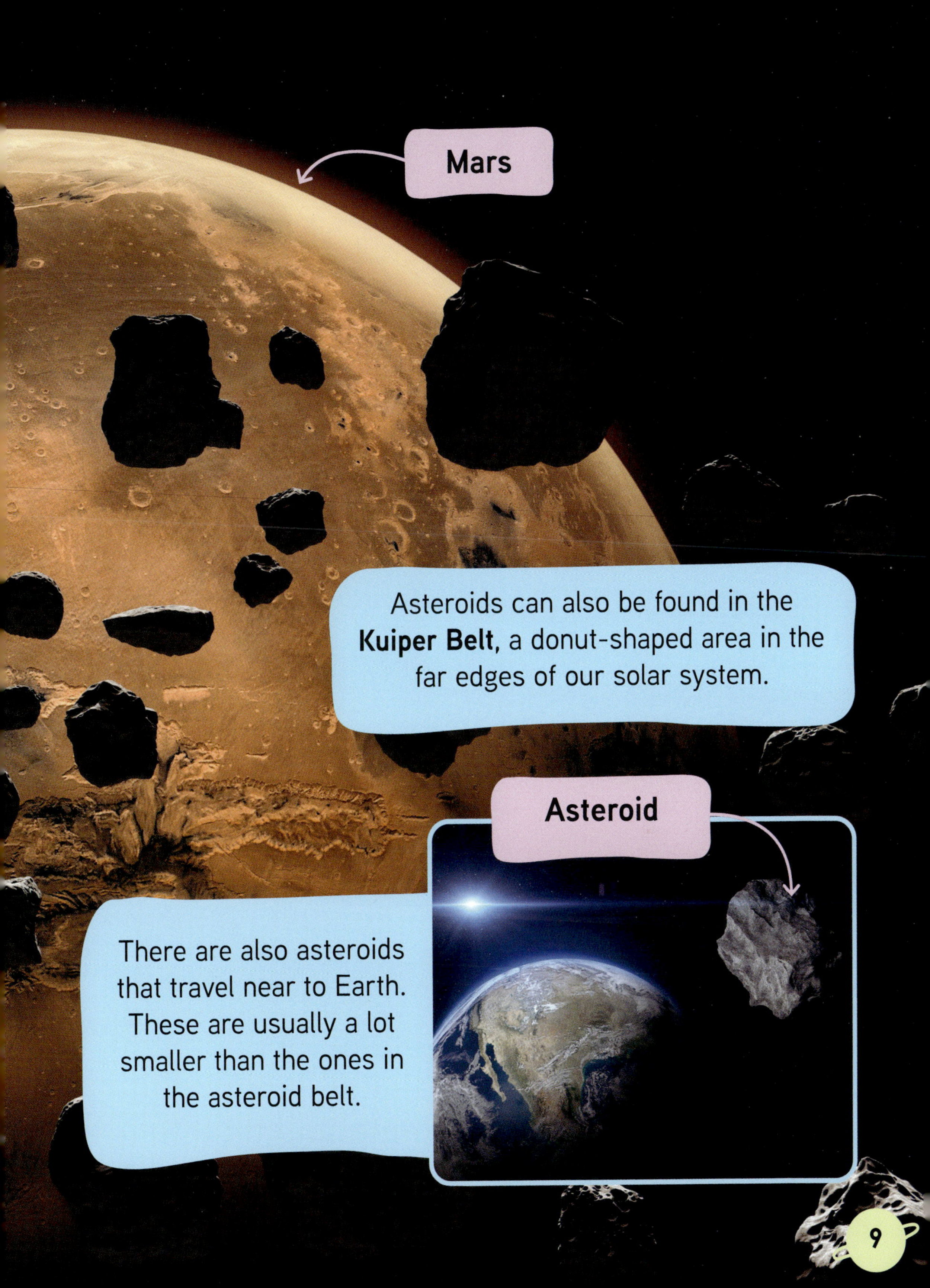

Asteroids can also be found in the **Kuiper Belt**, a donut-shaped area in the far edges of our solar system.

There are also asteroids that travel near to Earth. These are usually a lot smaller than the ones in the asteroid belt.

HUNTING FOR ASTEROIDS

Astronomers around the world are always looking for asteroids. Thousands of new ones are discovered each year!

Astronomers use **telescopes** to find them, even when they're still a huge distance away.

One important reason for astronomers to look for near-Earth asteroids is to spot any that might be on a collision-course with our planet!

Observatory

ASTEROIDS AND EARTH

Over the course of its history, Earth has been hit many times by asteroids.

Most asteroids are so small that they break up in Earth's atmosphere.

Meteor Crater, Arizona

But large ones can cause a lot of damage! They create huge **craters** in the ground.

It was an asteroid the size of a **mountain** that killed the dinosaurs!

WHAT IS A COMET?

Comets are objects that orbit the Sun. They are made mostly of ice, dust, and gases.

Their orbit around the Sun is shaped like an oval. Most of their time is spent at the very edges of the solar system. It takes them tens of thousands of years to fly close to the Sun!

When a comet finally does approach the Sun, the intense heat turns some of its dust and gas into two very long and bright "tails". We can see these from Earth!

FINDING COMETS

Astronomers believe that there is an area at the edge of our solar system called the **Oort Cloud**. This, as well as the Kuiper Belt, is where comets come from.

The Oort Cloud is like a giant bubble made of billions of icy objects that circle the entire solar system and everything in it. It's so far away that we can't photograph it, even using telescopes and **satellites**!

Voyager 1 has flown further from Earth than any other spacecraft. But it will still take 300 years to reach the beginning of the Oort Cloud, and another 30,000 years to emerge out the other side!

Voyager 1

WHAT CAN WE SEE?

Comets and asteroids are more difficult to spot than planets. They move a lot quicker across the night sky!

Sometimes small pieces of asteroids or comets can break off. If these small chunks fall through Earth's atmosphere, they leave a streak of light behind them in the sky. We call these "shooting stars"!

The most famous comet is called Halley's Comet. It can be spotted in the night sky every 76 years. Its next visit will be in 2061!

Halley's Comet

EXPLORING COMETS AND ASTEROIDS

Finding a comet or asteroid and launching a spacecraft to explore it while it flies around the solar system is very difficult. But it is possible!

The Philae spacecraft was the first to ever land on a comet! It helped scientists learn more about how comets are formed and what they are made of.

Philae spacecraft

NASA's DART spacecraft deliberately crashed into a moon orbiting an asteroid and changed its orbit. It showed that if an asteroid was heading towards Earth, we could knock it off-course!

NASA's DART spacecraft

WHAT'S NEXT?

Comets and asteroids may be small compared to the planets in our solar system, but there is still a lot to learn from them.

Asteroids sometimes contain a lot of **precious metals**. These could be used on Earth in everything, from computers to cars!

Precious metals

Comets from the Oort Cloud have been frozen for billions of years. Scientists studying them could learn a lot about what the solar system was like when it was formed!

GLOSSARY

Asteroid belt – an area between Mars and Jupiter where lots of space rocks can be found.

Asteroids – small space rocks that orbit the Sun.

Astronomers – scientists who study space.

Comets – objects made of dust and ice that orbit the Sun.

Craters – large holes that have been created by something hitting the ground.

Dwarf planet – a large, round object that orbits the Sun but isn't a moon or planet.

Gas – a substance that is neither solid nor liquid, and has no fixed shape. Many gases are invisible.

Kuiper Belt – a large area beyond Neptune where small, icy objects and asteroids can be found.

Moons – large, natural objects that orbit a planet.

Mountain – a rocky landform that rises high above its surrounding.

NASA – the National Aeronautics and Space Administration is an agency that deals with space exploration.

Oort Cloud – a huge 'bubble' of icy objects surrounding the solar system.

Orbit – the path taken by one object circling around another object in space.

Precious metals – metals like gold that are rare and worth a lot of money.

Satellites – things that orbit around a planet. They can be natural, like the Moon, or human-made.

Solar system – the Sun and everything that moves around it.

Telescopes – instruments that make far away objects appear bigger.

Picture credits:
(t=top; b=bottom; m=middle; l=left; r=right):

Wikipedia: By DLR, CC-BY 3.0, CC BY 3.0 de 20mr; By Moon image: Gregory H. ReveraCeres image: Justin CowartVesta image: NASA/JPL-Caltech/UCAL/MPS/DLR/IDA - File:FullMoon2010.jpgFile:Ceres - RC3 - Haulani Crater (22381131691).jpgFile:Vesta full mosaic.jpg, Public Domain 7tr; By NASA/JPL - http://solarsystem.nasa.gov/multimedia/display.cfm?IM_ID=2194 (file), Public Domain 17br; By NASA/W. Liller - NSSDC's Photo Gallery (NASA):http://nssdc.gsfc.nasa.gov/photo_gallery/photogallery-comets.htmlhttp://nssdc.gsfc.nasa.gov/image/planetary/comet/lspn_comet_halley1.jpg, Public Domain 19tr. NASA: images-assets.nasa.gov/image/PIA25329/PIA25329~orig.jpg 21br. Shutterstock: Buradaki 8-9bg, 9br; Elena11 6-7bg; gidenilson 4-5bg; Irinak 12-13bg; Jan Garbers 18-19bg; Marko ALiak Sandr 2-3bg; Mikael Damkier 13tl; Pavel chagochkin 24bg; Phawat 22mr; Sergey Nivens 20-21bg; Triff 1bg, 14-15bg, 16-17bg, 22-23bg; Xavier Gallego morell 10-11bg.